Ingredients

1 Spelling

Spellings come from spells. As any good dictionary will tell us, there are three kinds of spells.

* There is what we do when we write.

* There is a spell of time.

* And there is magic.

We learn spelling by taking time to discover the magic of writing words.

We begin here with the magic – take a look at these 26 little squiggles.

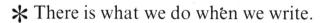

We turn them around and – *Hey Presto!* – we have all the letters of the alphabet.

We mix them all around, lots and lots of them. And – *Hey Presto* – we can make thousands upon thousands of different words:

> **kind** words – **bad** words – **sad** words – **happy** words –
> **funny** words – **fine** words – **easy** words – **hard** words
> **adjectives** – **nouns** – **verbs** – **adverbs** – **pronouns**
> **homophones** – **homonyms** – **palindromes** – **onomatopoeia**

There are so many words that no one person can possibly count them all, know them all or even spell them all.

But there is magic about them: the magic that helps everyone know so many of them so quickly, so that we hardly realize what is happening.

Fun with English

Good Spelling

WILLIAM EDMONDS

The author wishes to express his particular
gratitude to Robert Wheeler, the designer of all the
books in this series. There has been an especially
close collaboration at every stage and the author
has found this an immense stimulus and
encouragement. The author would also like to
thank Terry McKenna for his superbly amusing
illustrations, invaluable ingredients of the series.

KINGFISHER
Kingfisher Publications Plc
New Penderel House, 283–288 High Holborn,
London WC1V 7HZ

The material in this edition was previously published
by Kingfisher Publications Plc in the *Wordmaster* series
(1993) and in the *Guide to Good English* series (1989)

This edition published by Kingfisher Publications Plc 1999
10 9 8 7 6 5 4 3 2 1
1TR/0399/EDK/(ATL)/140EDI

A CIP catalogue record for this book is available from
the British Library

ISBN 0 7534 0367 6

Printed in Spain

Spelling is a **funny business**.

> Some people **love** it, some **people don't**.
> Sometimes it **comes**, sometimes it **won't**.
> Sometimes it is **fun**, or it is just **work** to be done
>
> but sometimes . . .
>
> it is simply MURDER

Some people are lucky. They pick up spelling without trying very hard at all.

Most of us have a bit of trouble in learning to spell. We have to work hard at it and put up with making lots of mistakes. But we usually learn to spell all right in the end.

Just a few of us have a terrible time with spelling. We have to work extra hard at it and then we still don't always get it right, even though we might be brilliant at other things such as reading, swimming or drawing.

In this book we want to give everybody another chance. We introduce a dozen different ways of learning how to spell. Readers can try each one and then see which ways suit them best. It is not a book to test you. It is a book for you to test.

But be careful! This book is dangerous. Keep it safe!

Words will stare you in the face. Your ears will deceive you. Rules will be broken. Spelling has magic power. No one can argue with good spelling.

Spelling is a very funny business. You are warned!

Read and spell

Can reading help you to spell?
Sometimes it does, sometimes it doesn't.
Let's see for ourselves!

Read the beginning of the last page once more and then see if you can put correct spellings in the spaces below.

Spelling is a funny _____

Some people _____ it, some _____

Sometimes it _____, sometimes it _____

Sometimes it is _____, or it is just _____ to be done.

But sometimes . . . it is simply _____

If you find this difficult read one line at a time slowly and out aloud.

If you find this easy, see how many of the different kinds of words (on page 5) you can write yourself.

Reading is good for meeting new spellings.
Reading is good for getting used to old spellings.
And reading is good – never mind the spellings.

Will you know these spellings tomorrow? That is the problem. But don't forget:

Reading is good for meeting new spellings.
Reading is good for getting used to old spellings.
And reading is good – never mind the spellings.

But reading is a funny business too, just like spelling.

Some people love reading. They like reading fast. They like racing on with stories. They don't always look carefully at each word. They can enjoy the stories and understand every little bit without having to study the spellings. They do it almost at a glance.

Some people read slowly. They look at each word with great care and sometimes puzzle over them if they look odd. You can't help noticing the spellings if you read like this. This is how many of us start reading.

If you read aloud to yourself or a friend, then you have to read quite slowly. Saying words is different from thinking them in your head. It makes you give them each a special sound. This is useful when you start writing because you often imagine yourself talking aloud as you write.

Now read these two lines:

> **Once upon a time there were two talking tortoises.**
>
> *Wunsapon a tym thair wer to torking tortussiz.*

Which line do you find easier to read?
Do you see how good spelling makes for good reading?
Reading and spelling help each other.

So, keep on reading. If you are a fast reader and a not-very-good speller try reading a little more slowly and, if possible, aloud.

Sound and spell

. . . found a **shell – bound** to **sell**

. . . hound on **mound – tell** by the **smell**

The 'ound' and 'ell' parts of these words always make the same sound. The sound parts of words can help us to spell well, especially when we are first learning to write.

We can all think of words with

ook sounds	or **end** sounds	or **old** sounds
cook	**lend**	**hold**
shook	**friend**	**sold**
t___	**m**___	**t**___
___	___	___
___	___	___

Sounds are often good for helping us to get the beginnings and ends of words right.

Think of words beginning with the *b* sound.

baked beans   butterflies   buns   b_____ **b**_____

Think of m words

mother   moon   magic   m_____ **m**_____ **m**_____

And think of '. . .ing' words:

singing   jumping _____**ing** _____**ing**

A few special words can make the sounds of sounds themselves:

Making these kinds of words is called **onomatopoeia**.

But, be careful with sounds!
There are sometimes different words which sound the same:

sea see   there their   hair hare   to two too

These don't look the same and nor, of course, do they mean the same thing.
These kinds of words are called **homophones.**

Then, again, there are words which can look the same but have quite different sounds and meanings. **Row,** for instance is a word you can have a **row** about when you are angry in a boat. **Lead** is another **misleading** word in this way, just like **refuse** which can be a question of obstinacy or rubbish. These kinds of words are called **homonyms**.

rowing row

← Lead →

The letters *ough* are especially **tough** for readers because they can have so many different sounds. They come in bakers' **dough,** on a **bough** of a tree and even **through thoroughly thoughtful coughing**. In each of these words the *ough* part makes a different sound.

So you see, we cannot always depend on the sounds of words to give us the right spellings.
Sounding does help us, but it is no good without looking as well.

Look and spell

When we talk we make sounds; they are there to be heard. When we write we usually make marks on paper; they are there to be seen. To be good at writing and spelling we have to be good at seeing.

Sometimes it helps to look at words in the same way as we look at pictures.

beautiful

Enjoy the beauty of the shape of each letter and see how it fits together with the ones next to it to make little patterns:

bea   eau   tif   ful

And enjoy the beauty of the shape of the whole word.

beautiful

No other word has exactly the same shape as this one. It is very special.

1 → **Look** long and hard at this picture again.

2 → Now **cover** it with your hand and try and see (**spell**) it in your mind.

3 → Take your hand away and **check** whether the picture in your mind was the same.

4 → If you were not sure try again.

LOOK ➡ COVER ➡ SPELL ➡ CHECK

This is a very simple and useful way of helping us to spell.

Try it in turn with each of these words. *(Use a pencil in case you don't get it right first time, and, if you like, write on a separate piece of paper)*.

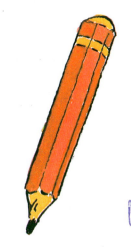

LOOK	COVER	SPELL	CHECK
bird	✓	bird	☑ ☑
beetle	✓	beetle	✓
beard	✓	beared	✗
bear	✓	bear	✓
ear	✓	ear	✓
eye	✓	eye	✓
word	✓	werd / word	✓
third	✓	3rd / third	

Sounding does not help very much in trying to remember these words, does it? They give us an important warning:

BE WISE – USE YOUR EYES!

DISCO SPIDERS

5 Look again and spell

The beauty of writing is that it stays. We can look at it again and again. There is always another chance to look, cover, spell and check. It does not matter how many times you keep on trying.

COKE

Sometimes a good way to start learning a new word is just to copy it letter by letter. Copy some of your favourite words into the boxes below!

Now make sure you know them:

LOOK ➡ COVER ➡ SPELL ➡ CHECK

PETS

BIRTHDAYS

HAMBURGERS

SWIMMING

BIRMINGHAM

CRISPS CHOCLATE

Does it look right?

SKATEBOARDS

If we keep on meeting words we begin to know if they look right or not. Sometimes it helps if we try writing words in two or three different ways to see which one looks right.

I ♥ spagetty

busness   busyness   business

I ♥ spaggetty

I ♥ Pasta

Can you tell which one of these looks right?

becaus   becos   (because)

Sataday (Saturday) Saterday

(School) scule   skool

seeling   ceeling   (ceiling)

dissappointment (disapointment) disappointment

Sepreyes   surprize (surprise)

Check in the index if you are not sure.

Look out! Look carefully! Look again!

ICE CREAM

CHIPS

PIZZA

Name and spell

The first word that many of us learn to write is our own name. Some names are easy – **Tom**, **Pat**, **Nan** or **Ben**. Others may be not so easy – **Elizabeth**, **Christopher**, **Cecilia** or **Nebuchadnezzar**.

Names are labels: we all have to use the same ones so that we can know who, what or where we are talking or writing about. It is important to get names right. It is bad manners to call somebody or some place by the wrong name. It is also bad manners not to write a name correctly or begin it with a capital letter.

Best friends

(Write their names here on a piece of paper).

Mother

Father

1

2

3

4

Look-Cover-Spell and Check

Keep your friends – Remember their names!

The right place

London   Washington   Paris   Timbuktu

Europe   Africa   America   Australia   Asia

Favourite place:

PARIS is named after a Greek King's Son

CAPITAL CAPITAL – Names of people, places and times

The right date

Days and months are tricky words. See a diary or calendar if you are not sure of any of them.

Monday
Moon day

Tuesday
TIWS day named after Saxon god

Wednesday
Wodensday named after Saxon god

Thursday
Thor's day named after Saxon god

Friday
Freya's day named after Saxon goddess

Saturday
Saturn's day named after Roman god

Sunday
named after the Sun

Do you see why **Wednesday** is not wensday?

We have to thank the Romans for the names of the months.

**January February March April May
June July August September October
November December**

Favourite Day:

Favourite Month:

JULY is named after Julius Caesar

always begin with capital letters.

7 Know and spell

1 Knowing words – Spelling out the meanings

Knowing the meanings of words is important for spelling. We learn meanings not just by hearing and seeing new words but especially by saying and writing them ourselves. When we do this they become *our* words with *our* meanings. By spelling them the right way we make ourselves clearly understood.

2 Knowing about words

There is a story behind the spelling of every word. English is really a mixture of words which have come from many different peoples and languages. It is a mixture which is always changing. The Saxons, the Angles, the Vikings, the Greeks, the Romans, the French and the American Indians are among the many peoples who have added words to the English language. That is why many spellings look peculiar to us now.

Greek words
drama comet medal grotto torso acrobat encyclopaedia and all those 'ology' (study of) words like psychology geology ornithology

Scottish Gaelic words
loch clan slogan whisky

Roman words
castle colonel infantry cavalry campaign.

Indian words
bungalow dungarees pyjamas curry

Welsh words
coracle flannel maggot eisteddfod

We can use some of the words that we have already met and give them special meanings of our own:

Nebuchadnezzar thought Wednesday was beautiful

Can you find ways of writing these other words in a sentence and making them yours?

Saturday business tough

or **February friend beard**

In a funny way the words with odd spellings can be the ones that most stick in our minds. See how many of these oddities stick with you. See, too, if you can make some of them your own by bringing them into a story or poem.

Italian words
piano umbrella balcony concert

German words
kindergarten hamburger pretzel plunder

French words
beef pork veal buffet café guillotine

Dutch words
golf aloof knapsack skipper yacht toy deck

Spanish words
cigar mosquito canyon rodeo alligator tornado.

American Indian words
canoe moose tepee tomahawk

You can find out more about different kinds of words in the **Kingfisher Guide to Words.**

Spell to rule

Rules are useful if they are simple and if there are not too many of them to remember. The trouble with spelling is that we can make hundreds of rules and they still don't always work.

But most good spellers keep a few rules in their mind and find that these are helpful.

So here are some rules that are often used. See which ones suit you best and which you find easiest to remember.

1 *i before e except after c – when the ie rhymes with dee*

**belief, chief, pier, sieve, field, piece,
ceiling, receive, receipt, deceit, conceive.**
Exceptions: **weird, seize, Keith.**

2 *Watch out for suffixes – extra bits added onto the ends of words: they often change the old ending.*

A *y changes to i or ie, except when it is after a vowel, and not before ing.*

**fly – flies, sky – skies, penalty – penalties,
happy – happily, merry – merrily,
early – earlier, ready – readiness,
day – days, boy – boys, monkey – monkeys,**
Exceptions: **day – daily, portray – portrait,
plenty – plenteous, miscellany – miscellaneous.**

a e i o u are vowels

B *words ending in e drop the e when they have a suffix beginning with a vowel or a y.*

stone – stony, inquire – inquiry,
care – caring, retire – retiring,
but **careful – careless, praise – praiseworthy**
Exceptions: **argument, awful, shoeing, hoeing.**

C *Words ending in a single consonant (other than w, x or y) after a single vowel will double this consonant when there is a suffix beginning with a vowel.*

commit – committee, forget – forgetting,
fit – fitting, fitter, fittest *but* **fitness, fitful**
occur – occurrence, occurred.
Exceptions: **buses, gases, developed, developing.**

D *When full is added to a word one of the 'l's is dropped.*

care – careful, peace – peaceful, thought – thoughtful
but we always write '. . . **fully'** *with 2 'l's.*
carefully, peacefully, thoughtfully.

3 Watch out for plurals!

A *The usual way to make numbers of nouns is to add s to the word.*

fire – fires, boy – boys, toe – toes

B *But nouns already ending in a hissing consonant (s, sh, ch, x, z) and most nouns ending in -o add es.*

bus – buses, match – matches, box – boxes, potato – potatoes
Exceptions: **solos, pianos, banjos.**

C *Some nouns ending in f change to -ves.*

leaf – leaves, wolf – wolves *Exceptions:* **chiefs, hoofs, roofs.**

9 Compute and spell

Can computers take away the pain and strain of learning to spell? They can and they can't.

■ **Computers can correct spelling mistakes.**

Computer spell-check programs are a wonderful invent<u>oin</u>*. Many computers now have word-processing programs which can correct the spellings of up to 80,000 words. There could be many times when a computer with a spell-check program like this might save you a lot of bother. But there are snags, especially when we are just learning to spell.

*The spell-check will automatically change this to **invention**.

SPELL CHECK PROGRAMS

– only work if you can spell quite well already. Our guesses have to be close for the computer to recognize what we are trying to write. It might correct *sossages* but might have difficulty with *sosijiz* for *sausages*.

– cannot correct mistakes which are just wrong words as when we write *our* for *are* or *hour*, *to* for *two* or *too* and so on. It is easy to make mistakes like this and there is no way that a computer can think these ones out.

– can't check all foreign words, special invented words or unusual speech dialects like the British Cockney habit of dropping 'h's – *ave an appy new year!*

Computers can give us confidence with writing.

Writing on a computer is called word-processing.

One of the advantages of word-processing is that it can lessen the worry about spelling. With the delete key DEL and the cursor → it is easy to correct spelling mistakes without making an untidy mess. Even if you do make a spelling mistake people can think it is just a typing mistake!

Computers can help us practise looking.

Practise Look and Spell routines again.

Look – word appears on screen
Cover – word disappears from screen
Spell – you type what you remember
Check – the computer gives a signal to say if you are right or if you have to try again.

Computers can have good spelling puzzles and games.

There are many computer games and problem solving programs which directly help spelling.

Adventure games will sometimes need us to remember spellings of clues and directions. We cannot go on with the adventure or game until we have got the word right.

10 Puzzle and spell

Puzzles make us think. That's why so many of us like them, so long as they are neither too hard nor too easy. Here is some brain teasing which might help us to think in a different way about spelling.

1 Crossword.
When the words cross over each other they check the spelling.

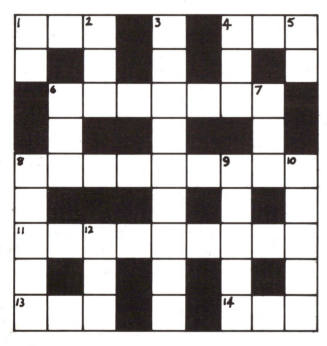

Across
1. The piper's son (3)
4. A precious stone (3)
6. (7)

8. Something said in anger (9)
11. (9)

13. What we breathe (3)
14. A large tree (3)

Down
1. . . . and fro (2)
2. Part of a Scottish name (3)
3. Puzzle like this (9)
4. A kind of antelope (3)
5. Myself (2)
6. Used for rowing (3)
7. Male teacher or knight (3)
8. Warm milky drink (5)
9. Girl or tree (5)
10. A sleep story (5)
12. Belonging to us (4)

2 A rebus rhyme
YYUR
YYUB
ICUR
YY4me.
(How should this rhyme really be written?)

3 Hidden animals

Can you see the animal hidden in each sentence?

(a) He came looking for trouble.
(b) They can be espied around the blossom.
(c) Impossible! O pardon me.
(d) Up I go.
(e) Well, I only got terrified out of my wits.
(2 animals)

4 Palindromes

What is the same about these names?

ANNA BOB ADA HANNAH

And what is peculiar about these sentences?

Madam I'm Adam.
God! a dog!
Step on no pets.

5 Anagram countries

(a) Erin lad
(b) Rain
(c) A tiger Ann
(d) Lop Dan
(e) Flan din
(f) Ada can

6 Mixed bags

See how many words you can make out of this mixed bag of letters.

m i x e d b a g

7 Mixed bags

See how many words you can make out of this mixed bag of word pieces.

*o pen to ed call car cil win e ful ly
bar w do sh s less hop and at here*

8 Food Chain

Sausageggsugaradish
(See how long you can make it)

Invent and spell

The key to all learning

★ Babies learn to talk by inventing words and new ways of saying them. They soon grow out of it but they have to start by finding out for themselves.

★ Young children often invent pretend-writing before they go to school. It makes them feel good and helps them to know what writing is about.

★ Spelling, too, has to begin with a lot of inventing. How can we possibly know it all before we begin?

Even when we are quite good at spelling there are still times when we have to invent or guess. Our invention might not be correct but it is often better to have a go than to wait for someone else to show us. Making mistakes is an important part of learning.

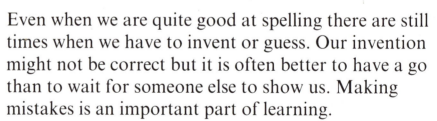

Sometimes our inventions can be **crazy** –

krehsee   craysy   creyzi

Making different crazy spellings can be fun and can sometimes help us to think about ways of spelling. Think of other crazy spellings for these words.

lunatic   daft   amazing   unbelievable

THE KEY TO SUCCESS

Complete inventions

Here are some new animals. Can you invent names for them? Maybe you can also make up the sounds that they make.

Whatever you **write** will be **right**. You invented these names and sounds yourself. These are the spellings which everybody else will now have to use for these creatures!

Getting it right

★ Good inventors know that with perseverance our inventions will get *beta* and *betta* and **better**.

★ Good inventors know that in the end they need to have good manners to make people notice their inventions. This means correct spellings. They make people think that you and your writing are important.

12 Search and spell

Dear Reader,

I have something to tell you. Actually, I am not brilliant at spelling myself. If I didn't have two dictionaries beside me and a patient wife who could answer all my questions I would not have been able to write this book.
    They have been wonderful. With their help I can now be certain that all the spellings are correct – except for the funny inventing bits. (I still can't be sure of remembering Nebuchadnezzar – thank goodness I haven't got a friend called that!)

I thought you ought to know my secret.

Yours sincerely,   William Edwards.

Hooray for Dictionaries!

Nearly every writer has a dictionary or two. Some writers use dictionaries to check spellings and meanings much more than others. It's their business. Nobody minds.

Dictionaries come in many different sizes and kinds.

pocket   compact   shorter   greater

Which one

Small dictionaries are useful for finding everyday spellings and meanings. Sometimes they have pictures to show the meanings of words. They are good for checking words which can easily be confused –

> **horse** *n* a four-legged animal with hooves . . .
> **hoarse** *adj.* of the voice, rough or croaking.

or the right place/plaice

> **place** *n* a particular area or location.
> **plaice** *n* a kind of flat fish.

When

Sometimes it is best to do all your writing quickly while the ideas are in your head and then check the spelling afterwards. Or sometimes it is best to use a dictionary as you write.

How

Dictionaries are good for making us concentrate on the order of letters in a word. Alphabetical order is a good way of sorting out words. Can you put these words in the order in which you find them in the dictionary?

**adjective achieve after alligator
acrobat adverb accommodation aloof**

Check the first words in the index to see whether your order is correct.

13 Remember and spell

One of the oldest ways of trying to remember spellings is to make lists and then learn the list by heart. When you think you have learned each list – maybe looking > covering > spelling > checking each word as you go along – get somebody to test you. This is a way that teachers often like to train our memories. It can be a good way of doing a little at a time – say a list or a half-list every day.

IMPORTANT

Make sure you choose or make a list that is right for you. It must be neither impossibly difficult nor too easy.

Here are a few lists for you to try. As you see there are many different ways of making groups of words. You can try and make some more.

starters	shopping	rhymes
good	sugar	fat
food	eggs	cat
get	biscuits	sat
wet	jam	flat
sad	honey	that
lad	bread	rat
bed	milk	spat
said	coffee	gnat

'pp's	teasers	homophones
pepper	knee	sale
stopped	key	sail
shopping	knife	piece
kipper	comb	peace
slipper	bomb	their
happy	gnome	there
disappointment	tongue	wood
apparatus	sign	would

'ough's	specials	story words
although	accommodation	once
cough	answer	upon
bought	because	there
brought	especially	was
through	mysterious	ugly
thorough	necessary	princess
thought	occur	happily
enough	unusual	after

?	'qu's	words from Greek
Who	quiet	alphabet
Why	quite	comet
When	squash	xylophone
How	square	telephone
Where	inquiry	geography
What	queen	archaeology
Whose	request	biology
Which	question	psychology

'i's & 'e's	extras	private specials
ceiling	exciting	_____
sieve	exaggerate	
niece	extraordinary	_____
achieve	excellent	
field	exercise	_____
receive	expensive	
deceit	extravagant	_____
friend	exquisite	

Fed up with testing? Why not try writing little nonsense rhymes or stories using some of the lists? It may be an even better way of remembering them.

14 The magic spell

Take each of the ingredients and taste them one by one before putting them in the pot.
Add some extra portions of the ones you particularly like.
Then slowly stir the whole mixture.

Let it brew!
Let the smell enter your nostrils!
Let the colours fill your eyes!
Let the hissing fill your ears!
Let the thoughts fill your mind!
Let the spell take its time!

Then *write* and *write* and *write*

Index

plenty, plenteous, 18
plunder, 17
pork, 17
portray, portrait, 18
potato, potatoes 19
praise, praiseworthy 19
princess, 29
psychology, 29
pyjamas, 17

queen, 29
question, 29
quiet, 29
quite, 29

ready, readiness, 18
receipt, 18
receive, 18
refuse, 9
request, 29
retire, retiring, 19
right, 25
rodeo, 17
roof, roofs, 19
row, 9

sail, 28
said, 28
sale, 28
Saturday, 13, 15, 17
sausages, 20
school, 13
sea, 9
see, 9
seize, 18
sell, 8
shoe, shoeing, 19
shopping, 28
shook, 8
sieve, 29
sign, 28
singing, 8
skipper, 17
slipper, 28
slogan, 17
sold, 8
solos, 19
square, 29
squash, 29
stone, stony, 19
sugar, 28
surprise, 13

talking, 7
tepee, 17
telephone, 29
tell, 8
that, 28
their, 9, 28
there, 7, 9, 28, 29
thoroughly, 9, 29
thought, thoughtful, 9, 17, 19, 29
through, 9, 29
time, 7
to, 9, 20
toe, toes, 19
tomahawk, 17
tongue, 28
too, 9, 20
torso, 16
toy, 17
two, 7, 9

ugly, 29
upon, 7, 29
umbrella, 17
unbelievable, 24
unusual, 29

veal, 17
verb, 4

was, 7, 29
Wednesday, 15, 17
weird, 18
were, 7
wet, 28
what, 29
when, 29
where, 29
which, 29
whisky, 17
who, 29
who's, 29
why, 29
wolf, wolves, 19
won't, 5, 6
work, 5, 6
would, 28
write, 25, 30

xylophone, 29

yacht, 17

Answers to pages 22 and 23

2 Too wise you are
  Too wise you be
  I see you are
  Too wise for me

3 (a) camel
  (b) bees
  (c) leopard
  (d) pig
  (e) lion & otter

4 **Palindromes**
  These are words or groups of words which read the same backwards as they do forwards.

5 (a) Ireland   (d) Poland
  (b) Iran   (e) Finland
  (c) Argentina   (f) Canada